SPRING

In emerald shoes Spring pirouettes
Upon a crystal stage;
Then lifts enchanting hands to free
A singing scarlet page.

From barren stalks she draws bright flags
As sun spotlights her art,
And with a violet-scented kiss
She melts King Winter's heart.

Louise Hajek

MARCH

Hear the madcap March winds run,
Bent on gay and boisterous fun;
Laughing, whistling, blustering, swirling,
Shrieking, blowing, twisting, whirling;
Rushing with a threatening roar,
Rattling casement, banging door;
Shaking, waking flower and tree,
Running wide and high and free;
Calling, shouting far and near:
"Wake up! Wake up! Spring is here!"

Katherine Edelman

APRIL

When was the sky
Ever blue as today?
When was the earth
Quite so mellow?
When was the song
Of the robin so gay?
Or the daffodil
So yellow?
How did we ever
Emerge from the snow?
March really was
Rather frightful,
When did April
Achieve such a glow?
When was the spring
More delightful?

Doris Chalma Brock

MAY

Do you remember back in childhood
How we loved the first of May
When we left our flower-filled baskets
On doorsteps, then ran away?
Do you remember how the gayest basket
Was for the one we loved the best,
And in it went the blossoms
That were fairer than the rest;
Such a beautiful and gracious custom
Somehow lost along the way,
But its memories come surging
As I welcome in the May.

Milly Walton

SUMMER

Quickly, Summer, safely gather
Every cherished bit of beauty
From each shortened day;
Examine each with tenderness
Before it's put away.
Hold the magic of your mornings
Guard your heaven's brilliant blue,
Lock the lazy haze of evening
Close against the warmth of you.
Pack each precious well-loved moment
Sprinkle it with sun sachet,
Safely, Summer, store them till
You gently shake them out next May.

Doris Chalma Brock

JUNE

And what is so rare as a day in June?
  Then, if ever, come perfect days;
Then Heaven tries earth if it be in tune,
  And over it softly her warm ear lays;
Whether we look or whether we listen,
We hear life murmur or see it glisten;
Every clod feels a stir of might,
  An instinct within it that reaches and towers,
And, groping blindly above it for light,
  Climbs to a soul in grass and flowers.

James Russell Lowell

JULY

The summer harvest day begun
With cloudless dawn and flaming sun;
Ripe grain the sickle flashes through;
The sweep of scythes in morning dew;
The nooning underneath the trees
Made cool by sea or mountain breeze;
The thundershower, the clearing sky,
And sunset splendor of July.

John Greenleaf Whittier

AUGUST

Above the slowly moving stream,
Half-sleepily on leaning boughs
Through midday hours
As in a dream
The tired leaves drowse.

Stirring, half-wakeful, now and then
To send a yellowing leaf to ride
In onward and
Unconscious course
Upon the listless watertide.

Katherine Edelman

AUTUMN

The year's last, loveliest smile.

William Cullen Bryant

SEPTEMBER

The goldenrod is yellow,
  The corn is turning brown,
The trees in apple orchards
  With fruit are bending down;

The gentian's bluest fringes
  Are curling in the sun;
In dusty pods the milkweed
  Its hidden silk has spun;

The sedges flaunt their harvest
  In every meadow nook,
And asters by the brookside
  Make asters in the brook.

From dewy lanes at morning
  The grapes' sweet odors rise;
At noon the roads all flutter
  With yellow butterflies--

By all these lovely tokens
  September's days are here,
With summer's best of weather
  And autumn's best of cheer.

Helen Hunt Jackson

OCTOBER

Where are you going, my children?
Down autumn's leaf-strewn lanes
To find Jack Frost who tiptoed by
And touched our windowpanes.
   I see storm windows that must be hung,
     You see frost tracings in early sun.
   I see the leaves to be raked in a mound,
     You see tumbling mats on the ground.
Where are you going, my children?
Just down the road a way
To see the tree where the hoot owl sits
And a field where rabbits play.
   I see small boots to be marked and mated,
     You see a world newly decorated.
   Oh, let me come with you down that lane
     And see October as a child again.

Barbara Burrow

NOVEMBER

November is a lonely waif
With wistful wide-eyed ways,
Subdued by the flamboyance of
The bright October days,
And feeling very small before
December's sparkling glance.
Never mind, November, twirl
Your tattered skirts and dance,
Dance a bittersweet ballet
With the leaves that fly away!

Doris Chalma Brock

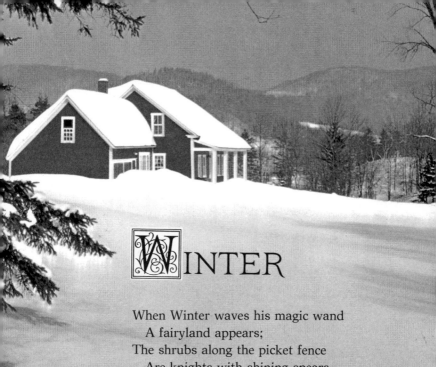

WINTER

When Winter waves his magic wand
  A fairyland appears;
The shrubs along the picket fence
  Are knights with shining spears.

The fountain is a crystal throne
  Where old King Jack Frost rules;
The evergreens are stately queens
  In silvery lace and jewels.

The fence-post sentinels at the gate,
  Whose hats are frosty globes
Command that all who enter here
  Be dressed in ermine robes.

Edith Powell Wortman

DECEMBER

Drifting downward through the sky, comes the glistening snow;
Floating, whirling, twirling by, down to earth below.
Snowflakes, snowflakes, large and small, far as eye can see;
Happy children, one and all, into the snowflakes flee!

Ben Wood

JANUARY

Branches shiver naked in the breeze
Above the silver wavelets of a rill,
Snow-white quilting hugs low round the trees
As winter flaunts her power and her skill.
Unlike emblazoned twilights of a May,
When angels finger-paint each amber cloud,
The January dusk is palest gray
Yet every bit as beautifully endowed

FEBRUARY

When February tires
Of her somber dress
She tucks ice diamonds in her hair
With charming carelessness...
Sometimes she enfolds herself
In cloak of ermine snow...
And always, at her waist she wears
A Valentine-red bow!

Mary R. Hurley

As though reluctant to retire
And yield her reign to eventide,
The setting sun turns into fire
And tints the countryside.
Then as she slowly sinks from sight,
She calmly calls the earth to rest
And gently tucks into the west
The coverlet of night.

Barbara Burrow